DATE DUE		
MAY 1 8 2000 APR 0 1 2008		
MAY 2 4 2000		
SEP 1 3 2000		
OCT 1 2 2002		
OCT 2 6 2002		
DEC 0 2 2003 APR 2 0 2006		
JUL 1 1 2007		
JUL 1 1 2007		

JIMMY'S BLUES

SELECTED POEMS

JAMES BALDWIN

Also by James Baldwin

Go Tell It on the Mountain
Notes of a Native Son
Giovanni's Room
Nobody Knows My Name
Another Country
The Fire Next Time
Nothing Personal (with Richard Avedon)
Blues for Mister Charlie
Going to Meet the Man
Tell Me How Long the Train's Been Gone
The Amen Corner
A Rap on Race (with Margaret Mead)
No Name in the Street
A Dialogue (with Nikki Giovanni)
One Day When I Was Lost
If Beale Street Could Talk
The Devil Finds Work
Little Man, Little Man. A Story of Childhood
(with Yoran Cazac)
Just Above My Head
The Evidence of Things Not Seen
The Price of the Ticket

JIMMY'S BLUES

SELECTED POEMS

JAMES BALDWIN

St. Martin's Press
New York

Library of Congress Cataloging-in-Publication Data

Baldwin, James.
    Jimmy's blues : selected poems / James Baldwin.
        p.   cm.
    ISBN 0-312-05104-2 (paperback)
    ISBN 0-312-44247-5 (hardcover)
    I. Title.
    [PS3552.A45]5   1990]
    811'.54—dc20   90-37243
                                                              CIP

Contents

JIMMY'S BLUES

SELECTED POEMS

JAMES BALDWIN

Staggerlee wonders

1

I always wonder
what they think the niggers are doing
while they, the pink and alabaster pragmatists,
are containing
Russia
and defining and re-defining and re-aligning
China,
nobly restraining themselves, meanwhile,
from blowing up that earth
which they have already
blasphemed into dung:
the gentle, wide-eyed, cheerful
ladies, and their men,
nostalgic for the noble cause of Vietnam,
nostalgic for noble causes,
aching, nobly, to wade through the blood of savages –
ah – !
Uncas shall never leave the reservation,
except to purchase whisky at the State Liquor Store.
The Panama Canal shall remain forever locked:
there is a way around every treaty.
We will turn the tides of the restless
Caribbean,

the sun will rise, and set
on our hotel balconies as we see fit.
The natives will have nothing to complain about,
indeed, they will begin to be grateful,
will be better off than ever before.
They will learn to defer gratification
and save up for things, like we do.

Oh, yes. They will.
We have only to make an offer
they cannot refuse.

This flag has been planted on the moon:
it will be interesting to see
what steps the moon will take to be revenged
for this quite breathtaking presumption.
This people
masturbate in winding sheets.
They have hacked their children to pieces.
They have never honoured a single treaty
made with anyone, anywhere.
The walls of their cities
are as foul as their children.
No wonder their children come at them with knives.
Mad Charlie man's son was one of their children,
had got his shit together
by the time he left kindergarten,
and, as for Patty, heiress of all the ages,

she had the greatest vacation
of any heiress, anywhere:

Golly-gee, whillikens, Mom, real guns!
and they come with a real big, black funky stud, too:
oh, Ma! he's making eyes at me!

Oh, noble Duke Wayne,
be careful in them happy hunting grounds.
They say the only good Indian
is a dead Indian,
but what I say is,
you can't be too careful, you hear?
Oh, towering Ronnie Reagan,
wise and resigned lover of redwoods,
deeply beloved, winning man-child of the yearning
    Republic,
from diaper to football field to Warner Brothers
        sound-stages,
be thou our grinning, gently phallic, Big Boy of all the ages!

Salt peanuts, salt peanuts,
for dear hearts and gentle people,
and cheerful, shining, simple Uncle Sam!

Nigger, read this and run!
Now, if you can't read,
run anyhow!

9

From Manifest Destiny
(*Cortez, and all his men*
silent upon a peak in Darien)
to A Decent Interval,
and the chopper rises above Saigon,
abandoning the noble cause
and the people we have made ignoble
and whom we leave there, now, to die,
one moves, With All Deliberate Speed,
to the South China Sea, and beyond,
where millions of new niggers
await glad tidings!

No, said the Great Man's Lady,
I'm against abortion.
I always feel that's killing somebody.
Well, what about capital punishment?
I think the death penalty helps.

That's right.
Up to our ass in niggers
on Death Row.

Oh, Susanna,
don't you cry for me!

2

Well, I guess what the niggers
is supposed to be doing
is putting themselves in the path
of that old sweet chariot
and have it swing down and carry us home.

That would *help*, as they say,
and they got ways
of sort of nudging the chariot.
They still got influence
with Wind and Water,
though they in for some surprises
with Cloud and Fire.

My days are not their days.
My ways are not their ways.
I would not think of them,
one way or the other,
did not they so grotesquely
block the view
between me and my brother.

And, so, I always wonder:
can blindness be desired?
Then, what must the blinded eyes have seen
to wish to see no more!

For, I have seen,
in the eyes regarding me,
or regarding my brother,
have seen, deep in the farthest valley
of the eye, have seen
a flame leap up, then flicker and go out,
have seen a veil come down,
leaving myself, and the other,
alone in that cave
which every soul remembers, and
out of which, desperately afraid,
I turn, turn, stagger, stumble out,
into the healing air,
fall flat on the healing ground,
singing praises, counselling
my heart, my soul, to praise.

What is it that this people
cannot forget?

Surely, they cannot be so deluded
as to imagine that their crimes
are original?

There is nothing in the least original
about the fiery tongs to the eyeballs,
the sex torn from the socket,
the infant ripped from the womb,

the brains dashed out against rock,
nothing original about Judas,
or Peter, or you or me: nothing:
we are liars and cowards all,
or nearly all, or nearly all the time:
for we also ride the lightning,
answer the thunder, penetrate whirlwinds,
curl up on the floor of the sun,
and pick our teeth with thunderbolts.

Then, perhaps they imagine
that their crimes are not crimes?

Perhaps.
Perhaps that is why they cannot repent,
why there is no possibility of repentance.
Manifest Destiny is a hymn to madness,
feeding on itself, ending
(when it ends) in madness:
the action is blindness and pain,
pain bringing a torpor so deep
that every act is willed,
is desperately forced,
is willed to be a blow:
the hand becomes a fist,
the prick becomes a club,
the womb a dangerous swamp,
the hope, and fear, of love

is acid in the marrow of the bone.
No, their fire is not quenched,
nor can be: the oil feeding the flames
being the unadmitted terror of the wrath of God.

Yes. But let us put it in another,
less theological way:
though theology has absolutely nothing to do
with what I am trying to say.
But the moment God is mentioned
theology is summoned
to buttress or demolish belief:
an exercise which renders belief irrelevant
and adds to the despair of Fifth Avenue
on any afternoon,
the people moving, homeless, through the city,
praying to find sanctuary before the sky
and the towers come tumbling down,
before the earth opens, as it does in *Superman*.
They know that no one will appear
to turn back time,
they know it, just as they know
that the earth has opened before
and will open again, just as they know
that their empire is falling, is doomed,
nothing can hold it up, nothing.
We are not talking about belief.

3

I wonder how they think
the niggers made, make it,
how come the niggers are still here.
But, then, again, I don't think they dare
to think of that: no:
I'm fairly certain they don't think of that at all.

Lord,
I watch the alabaster lady of the house,
with Beulah.
Beulah about sixty, built four-square,
biceps like Mohammed Ali,
she at the stove, fixing biscuits,
scrambling eggs and bacon, fixing coffee,
pouring juice, and the lady of the house,
she say, she don't know *how*
she'd get along without Beulah
and Beulah just silently grunts,
I reckon you don't,
and keeps on keeping on
and the lady of the house say,
She's just like one of the family,
and Beulah turns, gives me a look,
sucks her teeth and rolls her eyes
in the direction of the lady's back, and
keeps on keeping on.

While they are containing
Russia
and entering onto the quicksand of
China
and patronizing
Africa,
and calculating
the Caribbean plunder, and
the South China Sea booty,
the niggers are aware that no one has discussed
anything at all with the niggers.

Well. Niggers don't own nothing,
got no flag, even our names
are hand-me-downs
and you don't change that
by calling yourself X:
sometimes that just makes it worse,
like obliterating the path that leads back
to whence you came, and
to where you can begin.
And, anyway, none of this changes the reality,
which is, for example, that I do not want my son
to die in Guantanamo,
or anywhere else, for that matter,
serving the Stars and Stripes.
(I've *seen* some stars.
I *got* some stripes.)

Neither (incidentally)
has anyone discussed the Bomb with the niggers:
the incoherent feeling is, the less
the nigger knows about the Bomb, the better:
the lady of the house
smiles nervously in your direction
as though she had just been overheard
discussing family, or sexual secrets,
and changes the subject to Education,
or Full Employment, or the Welfare rolls,
the smile saying, *Don't be dismayed.*
We know how you feel. You can trust us.

Yeah. I would like to believe you.
But we are not talking about belief.

4

The sons of greed, the heirs of plunder,
are approaching the end of their journey:
it is amazing that they approach without wonder,
as though they have, themselves, become
that scorched and blasphemed earth,
the stricken buffalo, the slaughtered tribes,
the endless, virgin, bloodsoaked plain,
the famine, the silence, the children's eyes,
murder masquerading as salvation, seducing

every democratic eye,
the mouths of truth and anguish choked with cotton,
rape delirious with the fragrance of magnolia,
the hacking of the fruit of their loins to pieces,
hey! the tar-baby sons and nephews, the high-yaller
    nieces,
and Tom's black prick hacked off
to rustle in the crinoline,
to hang, heaviest of heirlooms,
between the pink and alabaster breasts
of the Great Man's Lady,
or worked into the sash at the waist
of the high-yaller Creole bitch, or niece,
a chunk of shining brown-black satin,
staring, staring, like the single eye of God:

creation yearns to re-create a time
when we were able to recognize a crime.

Alas,
my stricken kinsmen,
the party is over:
there have never been any white people,
anywhere: the trick was accomplished with mirrors –
look: where is your image now?
where your inheritance,
on what rock stands this pride?

Oh,
I counsel you,
leave History alone.
She is exhausted,
sitting, staring into her dressing-room mirror,
and wondering what rabbit, now,
to pull out of what hat,
and seriously considering retirement,
even though she knows her public
darc not let her go.

She must change.
Yes. History must change.
A slow, syncopated
relentless music begins
suggesting her re-entry,
transformed, virginal as she was,
in the Beginning, untouched,
as the Word was spoken,
before the rape which debased her
to be the whore of multitudes, or,
as one might say, before she became the Star,
whose name, above our title,
carries the Show, making History the patsy,
responsible for every flubbed line,
every missed cue, responsible for the life
and death, of all bright illusions
and dark delusions,

Lord, History is weary
of her unspeakable liaison with Time,
for Time and History
have never seen eye to eye:
Time laughs at History
and time and time and time again
Time traps History in a lie.

But we always, somehow, managed
to roar History back onstage
to take another bow,
to justify, to sanctify
the journey until now.

Time warned us to ask for our money back,
and disagreed with History
as concerns colours white and black.
Not only do we come from further back,
but the light of the Sun
marries all colours as one.

Kinsmen,
I have seen you betray your Saviour
(it is *you* who call Him Saviour)
so many times, and
I have spoken to Him about you,
behind your back.
Quite a lot has been going on

behind your back, and,
if your phone has not yet been disconnected,
it will soon begin to ring:
informing you, for example, that a whole generation,
in Africa, is about to die,
and a new generation is about to rise,
and will not need your bribes,
or your persuasions, any more:
nor your morality. Nor the plundered gold –
Ah! Kinsmen, if I could make you see
the crime is not what you have done to me!
It is you who are blind,
you, bowed down with chains,
you, whose children mock you, and seek another
master,
you, who cannot look man or woman or child in the
eye,
whose sleep is blank with terror,
for whom love died long ago,
somewhere between the airport and the safe-deposit
box,
the buying and selling of rising or falling stocks,
you, who miss Zanzibar and Madagascar and Kilimanjaro
and lions and tigers and elephants and zebras
and flying fish and crocodiles and alligators and
leopards
and crashing waterfalls and endless rivers,
flowers fresher than Eden, silence sweeter than the

grace of God,
passion at every turning, throbbing in the bush,
thicker, oh, than honey in the hive,
dripping
dripping
opening, welcoming, aching from toe to bottom
to spine,
sweet heaven on the line
to last forever, yes,
but, now,
rejoicing ends, man, a price remains to pay,
your innocence costs too much
and we can't carry you on our books
or our backs, any longer: baby,
find another Eden, another apple tree,
somewhere, if you can,
and find some other natives, somewhere else,
to listen to you bellow
till you come, just like a man,
but we don't need you,
are sick of being a fantasy to feed you,
and of being the principal accomplice to your
crime:
for, it is *your* crime, now, the cross to which you
cling,
your Alpha and Omega for everything.

Well (others have told you)

your clown's grown weary, the puppet master
is bored speechless with this monotonous disaster,
and is long gone, does not belong to you,
any more than my woman, or my child,
ever belonged to you.

During this long travail
our ancestors spoke to us, and we listened,
and we tried to make you hear life in our song
but now it matters not at all to me
whether you know what I am talking about – or not:
I know why we are not blinded
by your brightness, are able to see you,
who cannot see us. I know
why we are still here.

Godspeed.
The niggers are calculating,
from day to day, life everlasting,
and wish you well:
but decline to imitate the Son of the Morning,
and rule in Hell.

Song
(for Skip)

1

I believe, my brother,
that some are haunted by a song,
all day, and all the midnight long:

I'm going to tell
God
how you treated
Me:
one of these days.

Now, if that song tormented me,
I could have no choice but be
whiter than a bleaching bone
of all the ways there are,
this must be the most dreadful
way to be alone.

White rejects light
while blackness drinks it in
becoming many colours
and stone holds heat

while grass smothers
and flowers die
and the sleeping snakc
is hacked to pieces
while digesting his
(so to speak)
three-martini lunch.

Dread stalks our streets,
and our faces.
Many races
gather, again,
to despise and disperse
and destroy us:
nor can they any longer pretend
to be looking for a friend.
That dream was sold
when we were,
on the auction-block
of Manifest Destiny.

Time is not money.
Time
    is
        time.
And the time has come, again,
to outwit and outlast
survive and surmount

the authors of the blasphemy
of our chains.
At least, we know
a man, when we see one,
a shackle, when we wear one,
or a chain, when we bear one,
a noose from a halter,
or a pit from an altar.
We, who have been blinded,
are not blind
and sense when not to
trust the mind.

Time is not money.
Time is time.
You made the money.
We made the rhyme.

Our children are.
Our children are.
Our children are:
which means that we must be
the pillar of cloud by day
and of fire by night:
the guiding star.

2

My beloved brother,
I know your walk
and love to hear you
talk that talk
while your furrowed brow
grows young with wonder,
like a small boy, staring at the thunder.

I see you, somehow,
about the age of ten,
determined to enter the world of men,
yet, not too far from your mother's lap,
wearing your stunning
baseball cap.

Perhaps, then, around eleven,
wondering what to take as given,
and, not much later, going through
the agony bequeathed to you.

Then, spun around, then going under,
the small boy staring at the thunder.

Then, take it all
and use it well

this manhood, calculating
through this hell.

3

Who says better? Who knows more
than those who enter at that door
called back
for Black,
by Christians, who
raped your mother
and, then, lynched you,
seed from their loins,
flesh of their flesh,
bone of their bone:
what an interesting way
to be alone!

Time is not money:
time is time.
And a man is a man, my brother,
and a crime remains
a crime.

The time our fathers bought for us
resides in a place no man can reach
except he be prepared

to disintegrate himself into atoms,
into smashed fragments of bleaching bone,
which is, indeed, the great temptation
beckoning this disastrous nation.
It may, indeed, precisely, be
all that they claim as History.
Those who required, of us, a song,
know that their hour is not long.

Our children are
the morning star.

Munich, Winter 1973
(for Y.S.)

In a strange house,
a strange bed
in a strange town,
a very strange me
is waiting for you.

Now
it is very early in the morning.
The silence is loud.
The baby is walking about
with his foaming bottle,
making strange sounds
and deciding, after all,
to be my friend.

You
arrive tonight.

How dull time is!
How empty – and yet,
since I am sitting here,
lying here,
walking up and down here,

waiting,
I see
that time's cruel ability
to make one wait
is time's reality.

I see your hair
which I call red.
I lie here in this bed.

Someone teased me once,
a friend of ours —
saying that I saw your hair red
because I was not thinking
of the hair on your head.

Someone also told me,
a long time ago:
my father said to me,
It is a terrible thing,
son,
to fall into the hands of the living God.
Now,
I know what he was saying.
I could not have seen red
before finding myself
in this strange, this waiting bed.
Nor had my naked eye suggested

that colour was created
by the light falling, now,
on me,
in this strange bed,
waiting
where no one has ever rested!

The streets, I observe,
are wintry.
It feels like snow.
Starlings circle in the sky,
conspiring,
together, and alone,
unspeakable journeys
into and out of the light.

I know
I will see you tonight.
And snow
may fall
enough to freeze our tongues
and scald our eyes.
We may never be found again!

Just as the birds above our heads
circling
are singing,
knowing

that, in what lies before them,
the always unknown passage,
wind, water, air,
the failing light
the falling night
the blinding sun
they must get the journey done.
Listen.
They have wings and voices
are making choices
are using what they have.
They are aware
that, on long journeys,
each bears the other,
whirring,
stirring
love occurring
in the middle of the terrifying air.

The giver
(for Berdis)

If the hope of giving
is to love the living,
the giver risks madness
in the act of giving.

Some such lesson I seemed to see
in the faces that surrounded me.

Needy and blind, unhopeful, unlifted,
what gift would give them the gift to be gifted?
    The giver is no less adrift
        than those who are clamouring for the gift.

If they cannot claim it, if it is not there,
if their empty fingers beat the empty air
and the giver goes down on his knees in prayer
knows that all of his giving has been for naught
and that nothing was ever what he thought
and turns in his guilty bed to stare
at the starving multitudes standing there
and rises from bed to curse at heaven,
he must yet understand that to whom much is given
much will be taken, and justly so:
I cannot tell how much I owe.

3.00 a.m.
(for David)

Two black boots,
                on the floor,
figuring out what the walking's for.
Two black boots,
                now, together,
learning the price of the stormy weather.

To say nothing of the wear and tear
on
        the mother-fucking
                        leather.

The darkest hour

The darkest hour
is just before the dawn,
and that, I see,
which does not guarantee
power to draw the next breath,
nor abolish the suspicion
that the brightest hour
we will ever see
occurs just before we cease
to be.

Imagination

Imagination
creates the situation,
and, then, the situation
creates imagination.

It may, of course,
be the other way around:
Columbus was discovered
by what he found.

Confession

Who knows more
of Wanda, the wan,
    than I do?
And who knows more
of Terry, the torn,
    than I do?
And who knows more
    than I do
of Ziggy, the Zap,
fleeing the rap,
using his eyes and teeth
to spring the trap,
than I do!

    Or did.

Good Lord, forbid
    that morning's acre,
held in the palm of the hand,
one's fingers helplessly returning
dust to dust,
the dust crying out,
triumphantly,
    take her!

Oh, Lord,
     can these bones live?
I think, Yes,
then I think, No:
being witness to a blow
delivered outside of time,
witness to a crime
which time
is, in no way whatever,
compelled to see,
not being burdened with sight:
     like me.

     Oh, I watch Wanda,
Wanda, the wan,
     making love with her pots,
and her frying pan:
feeding her cats,
who, never, therefore,
dream of catching the rats
who bar
her not yet barred
and most unusual door.
The cats make her wan,
     a cat
(no matter how you cut him)
     not being a man,
     or a woman, either.

And, yet,
    at that,
better than nothing:
    But
nothing is not better than nothing:
nothing is nothing,
    just like
everything is everything
(and you better believe it).

    And,
Terry, the torn,
wishes he'd never been born
because he was found sucking a cock
in the shadow of a Central Park rock.
    The cock was black,
like Terry,
and the killing, healing,
thrilling thing
was in nothing resembling a hurry:
came, just before the cops came,
and was long gone,
baby,
out of *that* park,
while the cops were writing down Terry's name.

    Well.
Birds do it.

Bees endlessly do it.
Cats leap jungles
cages and ages
to keep on doing it
and even survive
    overheated apartments
    and canned cat-food
doing it to each other
all day long.
    It is one of the many forms of love,
and, even in the cat kingdom,
of survival:
    but Wanda never looked
    and Terry didn't think he was a cat
    and he was right about that.

    Enter Ziggy, the Zap,
having taken the rap
for a friend,
fearing he was facing the end,
but very cool about it,
he thought,
selling
what others bought
(he thought).

    But Wanda had left the bazaar
tricked by a tricky star.

She knew nothing of distance,
less of light,
the star vanished
and down came night.

Wanda thought this progression natural.
Refusing to moan,
she began to drink
far too alone
to dare to think.

I watch her open door.
She thinks that she wishes
to be a whore.
But whoredom is hard work,
stinks far too much of the real,
is as ruthless as a turning wheel,
and who knows more
of this
than I do?

Oh,
        and Ziggy, the Zap,
        who took the rap,
        raps on
to his fellow prisoners
in the cell he never left
and will never leave.

You'd best believe
it's cold outside.
Nobody
    wants to go where
    nothing is everything
    and everything adds up
    to nothing.

Better to slide
into the night
cling to the memory
of the shameful rock
which watched as the shameful act occurred
yet spoke no warning
said not a word.

    And who knows more
    of shame, and rocks,
    than I do?

Oh,
    and Wanda, the wan,
    will never forgive her sky.
    That's why the old folks say
    (*and who knows better than I?*)
    we will understand it
    better
    by and by.

My Lord.
I understand it,
now:
the why is not the how.

My Lord,
Author of the whirlwind,
and the rainbow,
Co-author of death,
giver and taker of breath
(Yes, every knee must bow),
I understand it
now:
the why is not the how.

Le sporting-club de Monte Carlo
(for Lena Horne)

The lady is a tramp
    a camp
    a lamp

The lady is a sight
    a might
    a light
the lady devastated
an alley or two
reverberated through the valley
which leads to me, and you

the lady is the apple
of God's eye:
He's cool enough about it
but He tends to strut a little
when she passes by

the lady is a wonder
daughter of the thunder
smashing cages
legislating rages
with the voice of ages
singing us through.

Some days
(for Paula)

1

Some days worry
some days glad
some days
more than make you
mad.
Some days,
some days, more than
shine:
when you see what's coming
on down the line!

2

Some days you say,
oh, not me never – !
Some days you say
bless God forever.
Some days, you say,
curse God, and die
and the day comes when you wrestle

with that lie.
       Some days tussle
then some days groan
and some days
don't even leave a bone.
Some days you hassle
all alone.

3

I don't know, sister,
what I'm saying,
nor do no man,
if he don't be praying.
I know that love is the only answer
and the tight-rope lover
the only dancer.
When the lover come off the rope
today,
the net which holds him
is how we pray,
and not to God's unknown,
but to each other – :
the falling mortal is our brother!

4

Some days leave
some days grieve
some days you almost don't believe.
Some days believe you,
some days don't,
some days believe you
and you won't.
Some days worry
some days mad
some days more than make you
glad.
Some days, some days,
more than shine,
witnesses,
coming on down the line!

Conundrum (on my birthday)
(for Rico)

Between holding on,
and letting go,
I wonder
how you know
the difference.

It must be something like
the difference
between heaven and hell
but how, in advance,
can you tell?

If letting go
is saying no,
then what is holding on
saying?
  Come.
  Can anyone be held?
  Can I – ?
The impossible conundrum,
the closed circle,
why
does lightning strike this house

and not another?
Or, is it true
that love is blind
until challenged by the drawbridge
of the mind?

But, saying that,
one's forced to see one's definitions
as unreal.
We do not know enough about the mind,
   or how the conundrum of the imagination
dictates, discovers,
or can dismember what we feel,
   or what we find.

Perhaps
one must learn to trust
one's terror:
the holding on
the letting go
is error:
   the lightning has no choice,
      the whirlwind has one voice.

Christmas carol

Saul,
how does it feel
to be Paul?
I mean, tell me about that night
you saw the light,
when the light knocked you down.
What's the cost
of being lost
and found?

It must be high.
And I've always thought you must have been,
stumbling homeward,
trying to find your way out of town
through all those baffling signals,
those one-way streets,
merry-making camel drivers
(complete with camels;
camels complete with loot)
going *root-a-toot-toot!*
before, and around you
and behind.
No wonder you went blind.

Like man, I can dig it.
Been there myself: you know:
it sometime happen so.
And the stink make you think
because you can't get away
you are surrounded
by the think of your stink,
unbounded.
And not just in the camels
and the drivers
and not just in the hovels
and the rivers
and not just in the sewers
where you live
and not just in the shit
beneath your nose
and not just in the dream
of getting home
and not just in the terrifying hand
which holds you tight,
forever to the land.
On such a night,
oh, yes,
one might lose sight,
fall down beneath the camels,
and see the light.

Been there myself: face down

in the mud
which rises, rises, challenging
one's mortal blood,
which courses, races, faithless,
anywhere,
which, married with the mud,
will dry at noon
soon.

Prayer
changes things.

It do.
If I can get up off this slime,
if I ain't trampled,
I will put off my former ways
I will deny my days
I will be pardoned
and I will rise
out of the camel piss
which stings my eyes
into a revelation
concerning this doomed nation.

From which I am, henceforth,
divorced forever!
Set me upon my feet,
my Lord,

I am delivered
out of the jaws of hell.
My journey splits my skull,
and, as I rise, I fall.

Get out of town.
This ain't no place to be alone.

Get past the merchants, and the shawls,
the everlasting incense: stroke your balls,
be grateful you still have them;
touch your prick
in a storm of wondering abnegation:
it will be needed no longer,
the light being so much stronger.

Get out of town
Get out of town
Get out of town

And don't let nobody
turn you around.

Nobody will: for they see, too,
 how the hand of the Lord has been laid on you.
    Ride on!
Let the drivers stare
and the camel's farts define the air.

Ride on!
Don't be deterred, man,
for the crown ain't given to the also-ran.

Oh, Saul,
how does it feel to be Paul?

Sometimes I wonder about that night.
One does not always walk in light.
My light is darkness
and in my darkness moves, forever,
the dream or the hope or the fear of sight.

Ride on!
        This hand, sometimes, at the midnight hour,
yearning for land, strokes a growing power,
true believer!
        Will he come again?
When will my Lord send my roots rain?
Will he hear my prayer?
        Oh, man, don't fight it
Will he clothe my grief?
        Man, talk about it
That night, that light
        Baby, now you coming.
I will be uncovered, on that morning,
        And I'll be there.

No tongue can stammer
nor hammer ring
no leaf bear witness
to how bright is the light
of the unchained night
which delivered
Saul
to Paul.

A lady like landscapes
(for Simone Signoret)

A lady like landscapes,
wearing time like an amusing shawl
thrown over her shoulders
by a friend at the bazaar:

Every once in a while she turns in it
just like a little girl,
this way and that way:

Regarde.
Ça n'était pas donné bien sûr
mais c'est quand même beau, non?

Oui, Oui.
Et toi aussi.
Ou plutôt belle
since you are a lady.

It is impossible to tell
how beautiful, how real, unanswerable,
becomes your landscape as you move in it,
how beautiful the shawl.

Guilt, Desire and Love

At the dark street corner
where Guilt and Desire
are attempting to stare
each other down
(presently, one of them
will light a cigarette
and glance in the direction
of the abandoned warehouse)
Love came slouching along,
an exploded silence
standing a little apart
but visible anyway
in the yellow, silent, steaming light,
while Guilt and Desire wrangled,
trying not to be overheard
by this trespasser.

Each time Desire looked towards Love,
hoping to find a witness,
Guilt shouted louder
and shook them hips
and the fire of the cigarette
threatened to burn the warehouse down.

Desire actually started across the street,
time after time,
to hear what Love might have to say,
but Guilt flagged down a truckload
of other people
and knelt down in the middle of the street
and, while the truckload of other people
looked away, and swore that they
didn't see nothing
and couldn't testify nohow,
and Love moved out of sight,
Guilt accomplished upon the standing body
of Desire
the momentary, inflammatory soothing
which seals their union
(for ever?)
and creates a mighty traffic problem.

Death is easy
(for Jefe)

1

Death is easy.
One is compelled to understand
that moment
which, anyway, occurs
over and over and over.
Lord,
sitting here now,
with my boy with a toothache
in the bed yonder,
asleep, I hope,
and me, awake,
so far away,
cursing the toothache,
cursing myself,
cursing the fence
of pain.

2

Pain is not easy;
reduces one to

toothaches
which may or may not
be real,
but which are real
enough
to make one sleep,
or wake,
or decide
that death is easy.

3

It is dreadful to be
so violently dispersed.
To dare hope for nothing,
and yet dare to hope.
To know that hoping
and not hoping
are both criminal endeavours,
and, yet, to play one's cards.

4

If
I could tell you
anything about myself:

if I knew something
useful – :
if I could ride,
master,
the storm of the unknown
me,
well, then, I could prevent
the panic of toothaches.
If I knew
something,
if I could recover
something,
well, then,
I could kiss the toothache
away,
and be with my lover,
who doesn't, after all,
like toothaches.

5

Death is easy
when,
if,
love dies.
Anguish is the no-man's-land
focused in the eyes.

Mirrors
(for David)

1

Although you know
what's best for me,
I cannot act on what you see.
I wish I could:
I really would,

     and joyfully,
act out my salvation
with your imagination.

2

Although I may not see your heart,
or fearful well-springs of your art,
I know enough to stare
down danger, anywhere.
I know enough to tell
you to go to hell
and when I think you're wrong
I will not go along.
I have a right to tremble

when you begin to crumble.
Your life is my life, too,
and nothing you can do
will make you something other
than my mule-headed brother.

A Lover's Question

   My country,
t'is of thee
I sing.

You, enemy of all tribes,
known, unknown, past,
present, or,
perhaps, above all,
to come:
I sing:
my dear,
            my darling,
jewel
(*Columbia, the gem of
the ocean!*)
or, as I, a street nigger,
would put it—:
(Okay. I'm *your* nigger
baby, till I get bigger!)
You are my heart.

Why
have you allowed yourself
to become so *grinly* wicked?

I
do not ask you why
you have spurned,
despised my love
as something beneath you.
We all have our ways and
days
but my love has been as constant
as the rays
coming from the earth
or the sun,
which you have used to obliterate
me,
and, now, according to your purpose,
all mankind,
from the nigger, to you,
and to your children's children.

I have endured your fire
and your whip,
your rope,
and the panic from your hip,
in many ways, false lover,
yet, my love:
you do not know
how desperately I hoped
that you would grow
not so much to love me
as to know
that what you do to me
you do to you.

No man can have a harlot
for a lover
nor stay in bed forever
with a lie.
He must rise up
and face the morning sky
and himself, in the mirror
of his lover's eye.

You do not love me.
I see that.
You do not see me:
I am your black cat.

You forget
that I remember an Egypt
where I was worshipped
where I was loved.

No one has ever worshipped you,
nor ever can: you think that love
is a territorial matter,
and racial,
oh, yes,
where I was worshipped
and you were hurling stones,
stones which you have hurled at me,
to kill me,
and, now,
you hurl at the earth,

our mother,
the toys which slaughtered
Cain's brother.

What panic makes you
want to die?
How can you fail to look
into your lover's eye?

Your black dancer
holds the answer:
your only hope
beyond the rope.

Of rope you fashioned,
usefully,
enough hangs from
your hanging tree
to carry you
where you sent me.

And, then, false lover,
you will know
what love has managed
here below.

Inventory/On Being 52

My progress report
concerning my journey to the palace of wisdom
is discouraging.
I lack certain indispensable aptitudes.
Furthermore, it appears
that I packed the wrong things.
I thought I packed what was necessary,
or what little I had:
but there is always something one overlooks,
something one was not told,
or did not hear.

Furthermore,
some time ago,
I seem to have made an error in judgment,
turned this way, instead of that,
and, now, I cannot radio my position.
(I am not sure that my radio is working.
No voice has answered me for a long time now.)

How long?
I do not know.

It may have been
that day, in Norman's Gardens,
up-town, somewhere,
when I did not hear
someone trying to say: I love you.
I packed for the journey in great haste.
I have never had any time to spare.
I left behind me
all that I could not carry.

I seem to remember, now,
a green bauble, a worthless stone,
slimy with the rain.
My mother said that I should take it with me,
but I left it behind.
(The world is full of green stones, I said.)

Funny
that I should think of it now.
I never saw another one like it—:
now, that I think of it.

There was a red piece of altar-cloth,
which had belonged to my father,
but I was much too old for it,
and I left it behind.

There was a little brown ball,
belonging to a neighbor's little boy.
I still remember his face,
brown, like the ball, and shining like the sun,
the day he threw it to me
and I caught it
and turned my back, and dropped it,
and left it behind.

I was on my way.
Drums and trumpets called me.
My universe was thunder.
My eye was fixed
on the far place of the palace.

But, sometimes, my attention was distracted
by this one, or that one,
by a river, by the cry of a child,
the sound of chains,
of howling. Sometimes
the wings of great birds
flailed my nostrils,
veiled my face, sometimes,
from high places, rocks fell on me,
sometimes, I was distracted by my blood,
rushing over my palm,
fouling the lightning of my robe.

My father's son
does not easily surrender.

My mother's son
pressed on.

Then,
I began to imagine a strange thing:
the palace never came any closer.
I began, nervously, to check
my watch, my compass, the stars:
they all confirmed
that I was almost certainly where I should be.
The vegetation was proper
for the place, and the time of year.
The flowers were dying,
but that, I knew,
was virtual, at this altitude.
It was cold,
but I was walking upward, toward the sun,
and it was silent, but—
silence and I have always been friends.

Yet—
my journey's end seemed
farther
than I had thought it would be.

I feel as though I have been badly bruised.
I hope that there is no internal damage.
I seem to be awakening
from a long, long fall.

My radio will never work again.
My compass has betrayed me.
My watch has stopped.

Perhaps
I will never find my way to the palace.
Certainly,
I do not know which way to turn.

My progress has been
discouraging.

Perhaps
I should locate the turning
and then start back
and study the road I've travelled.
Oh, I was in a hurry,
but it was not, after all,
if I remember,
an ugly road at all.
Sometimes, I saw
wonders greater than any palace,
yes,
and, sometimes, joy leaped out,
mightier than the lightning of my robe,
and kissed my nakedness.
Songs
came out of rocks and stones and chains,
wonder baptized me,
old trees sometimes opened, and let me in,

and led me along their roots,
down, to the bottom of the rain.

The green stone,
the scarlet altar-cloth,
the brown ball, the brown boy's face,
the voice, in Norman's Gardens,
trying to say: I love you.

Yes.
My progress has been discouraging.
But I think I will leave the palace where it is.
It has taken up quite enough of my time.
The compass, the watch, and the radio:
I think I will leave them here.
I think I know the road, by now,
and, if not, well, I'll certainly think of something.
Perhaps the stars will help,
or the water,
a stone may have something to tell me,
and I owe a favor to a couple of old trees
And what was that song I learned from the river
on one of those dark days?
If I can remember the first few notes
Yes
I think it went something like
Yes
It may have been the day I met the howling man,

who looked at me so strangely.
He wore no coat.
He said perhaps he'd left it at Norman's Gardens,
up-town, someplace.
Perhaps, this time, should we meet again, I'll
stop and rap a little.
A howling man may have discovered something I should know,
something, perhaps, concerning my discouraging progress.

This time, however,
hopefully,
should the voice hold me to tarry,
I'll be given what to carry.

Amen

No, I don't feel death coming.
I feel death going:
having thrown up his hands,
for the moment.

I feel like I know him
better than I did.
Those arms held me,
for a while,
and, when we meet again,
there will be that secret knowledge
between us.